POCKET BIGGIE WISDOM

POCKET BIGGIE WISDOM

INSPIRATIONAL QUOTES AND WISE WORDS FROM THE NOTORIOUS B.I.G.

Hardie Grant

BOOKS

"

TIME HEALS ALL WOUNDS, BUT THIS ONE AIN'T HEALED YET.

"

—Puff Daddy

CONT

ENTS

WHEN

G WAS LITTLE

"

I WAS A SNEAKY MOTHERF***KER, I GUESS.

"

"

**I ALWAYS BEEN MY OWN
PERSON. I KNOW WHAT
I WANTED TO DO SINCE THE
DAY I STEPPED IN THE GAME.**

"

On his dad:

"

I DIDN'T KNOW HIM AND I DON'T WANT TO KNOW HIM. MOMS SHOULD HAVE JUST PUSHED HIM OFF AND NOT EVEN HAD ME IF HE WASN'T GOING TO HANDLE HIS BUSINESS.

"

"

**I WAS REAL, REAL BAD.
YOU KNOW WHAT MADE IT
WORSE? MOTHERF***KERS
WOULD TELL MY MOTHER THAT
I DID SOMETHING, AND SHE
JUST WOULDN'T BELIEVE THEM.
'NOT MY CHRISTOPHER',
SHE WOULD SAY.**

"

"

I COULDN'T BRING
ANY OF MY CLOTHES TO THE
HOUSE, 'CAUSE MY MOMS
WOULD FLIP ...

... I USED TO HIDE ALL MY
S**T ON THE ROOF OF OUR
BUILDING, LEAVE FOR SCHOOL
IN THE BUSTED S**T MY MOMS
GAVE ME, AND CHANGE MY
WHOLE OUTFIT ON THE ROOF.

"

"

**I LIKED TO DRAW, BUT
WHAT COULD I DO WITH IT?
MAYBE I COULD BE AN ART
DEALER — NAH, I CAN'T SEE
MYSELF DOING THAT ...**

... MAYBE I COULD DO COMMERCIAL ARTS? BUT ONCE I GOT INTRODUCED TO THE CRACK GAME — COMMERCIAL ARTS? PLEASE.

"

"

**HOW REAL CAN YOUR
MUSIC BE IF YOU WAKE UP IN
THE MORNING HEARING BIRDS
AND CRICKETS? I NEVER HEAR
BIRDS WHEN I WAKE UP …**

... JUST A LOT OF CONSTRUCTION WORK, THE SMELL OF CHINESE TAKEOUT, CHILDREN SCREAMING, AND EVERYBODY KNOCKING A DIFFERENT TRACK FROM *READY TO DIE* AS THEY PASS DOWN THE STREET.

"

"

BROOKLYN IS THE LOVE BOROUGH. EVERYWHERE YOU GO, WE'RE ALREADY THERE.

"

"

MY TEMPER BE F**KIN' ME UP SOMETIMES. I OFTEN HAVE TO TELL MYSELF, 'WATCH WHAT YOU DOING, BIG, CAUSE YOU'RE NOT ON FULTON STREET ANYMORE.'

"

"

MY MENTALITY WAS MORE ABOUT GETTING PAPER, NOT DEALING WITH ANYTHING ELSE. NOT CARING ABOUT NOTHING, JUST WANTING TO GET MINE.

"

"

I PICKED UP THE MIKE AND RHYMED AND THEY WERE LIKE *'DAMN*, HE'S NICE.'

"

"

I KNEW I DIDN'T WANT TO BE THE CORNER GHETTO RAPPER. WHEN I HAD MY DREAMS OF GETTING INTO THE GAME IT WASN'T JUST TO GET IN THE GAME AND STILL BE ON THE CORNER ...

... I WANTED TO GET IN THE GAME AND GET THE BIG HOUSE, THE BIG CARS AND THE POOL AND DO ALL OF THAT.

"

BEHIND THE LY

"

WHEN I SAY I'M READY TO DIE, PEOPLE MAY BE, LIKE, 'OH, HE'S ON SOME KILLING-HIMSELF S**T.' THAT'S NOT WHAT I MEANT ...

... I MEANT THAT I WAS WILLING TO GO ALL OUT A HUNDRED PER CENT AS FAR AS THE MUSIC WAS CONCERNED.

"

"

I WAS NEVER ONE TO SAY THAT ALL MY RHYMES WERE MY EXACT LIFE EXPERIENCE.

"

"

THE WAY I WAS FEELING WHEN I DID *READY TO DIE* WAS LIKE I WAS ALREADY DEAD.

"

"

WHEN I WAS WRITING STUFF LIKE 'F**K THE WORLD, F**K MY MOMS AND F**K MY GIRL,' I WAS DEAD, MAN. THERE WAS NOTHING BUT ANGER COMING OUT ...

… NOTHING BUT ANGER.
BUT NOW, I CAN'T DO THAT
NO MORE. PEOPLE KNOW THAT
BIGGIE AIN'T ON THE CORNER
SELLING DRUGS ANYMORE.
WHY WOULD ANYONE WANT
TO HEAR ABOUT THAT?

"

"

WHEN I DID *READY TO DIE* IT WAS REAL BUT IT WAS REAL ANGRY. *LIFE AFTER DEATH* IS THE FLIP-SIDE — I CAN'T RHYME ABOUT BEING BROKE NO MORE BECAUSE I'M NOT BROKE ...

... I CAN'T RHYME ABOUT HUSTLIN' IN THE STREETS BECAUSE I'M NOT HUSTLIN' NO MORE.

"

"

I'M STILL SHY, I'M A QUIET DUDE. I USE MY VOICE TO SAY THE THINGS I WANT TO SAY IN MY MUSIC.

"

"

I'M JUST A NARRATOR,
I'M JUST TELLING THE STORY.

"

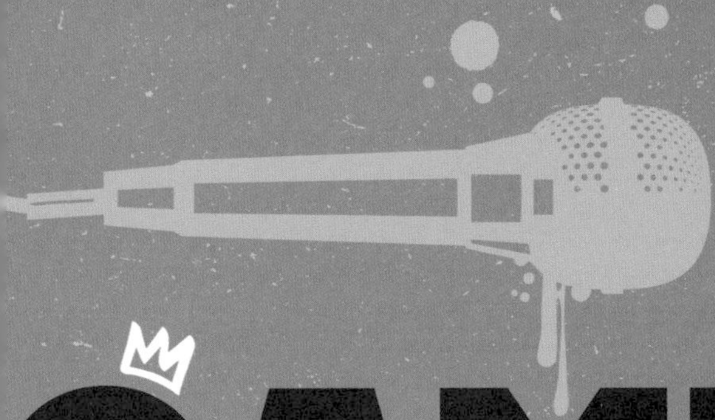

GAME

"

RIGHT NOW I'M JUST TRYING TO MASTER THIS RAP GAME A LITTLE BIT TIGHTER.

"

"

I'M MAKING MUSIC
FOR THE PEOPLE.

"

On his first meeting with Puff:

"

PUFF TOLD ME, 'IT SOUNDS LIKE YOU COULD RHYME FOREVER. I WANT TO SIGN YOU.'

"

On the black panther in the 'Hypnotise' video:

"

THEY BETTER LET THAT CAT KNOW WHO'S RUNNING THIS VIDEO. I'M ABOUT TO CALL MY BARBER AND HAVE HIM CUT MY INITIALS INTO HIS FUR.

"

"

IT'S A FUNNY THING — I KIND
OF REALISED HOW BIG TUPAC
AND I WAS, BECAUSE WE TWO
INDIVIDUAL PEOPLE, WE
WAGED A COASTAL BEEF ...

… ONE MAN AGAINST ONE MAN MADE A WHOLE WEST COAST HATE A WHOLE EAST COAST, AND VICE VERSA. AND THAT REALLY BUGGED ME OUT.

"

On selling out:

"

I'M NOT SCARED OF THAT ANYMORE, I HEAR SO MUCH OF WHAT'S GOING ON FROM PEOPLE COMING TO MY HOUSE —THEY'LL JUST TELL ME AN ILL STORY AND I CAN BUILD THAT INTO SOMETHING ...

THE RAP GAME

... I WAS NEVER ONE TO SAY
THAT ALL MY RHYMES WERE
MY EXACT LIFE EXPERIENCE.

"

49

"

I KNOW THAT TO [GET IN THE GAME] THERE WERE CERTAIN THINGS YOU HAD TO DO, YOU CAN PINCH IT OFF AND JUST ADD YOUR FLAVOUR TO IT …

... LINKING UP WITH PUFF
TO USE THE OLD FAMILIAR
TRACKS, THAT'S GONNA
GET THE ADULT ATTENTION
AND THE LYRICS GONNA GET
THE YOUNGER ATTENTION.
BLEND THEM BOTH.

"

On why he didn't rhyme about Tupac's death:

"

AFTER TUPAC'S DEATH I WAS MORE IN THE MIND FRAME TO KEEP MY BIG MOUTH SHUT. DON'T FEED INTO IT — IF YOU FEED INTO IT IT'S GONNA DO NOTHING BUT ESCALATE.

"

"

ALL I KNOW IS GOLD AND PLATINUM, AND I WANT TO BE PLATINUM. I'M JUST TRYING TO BLOW UP.

"

"

ONCE YOU ACHIEVE THE SUCCESS THAT YOU WANT, THAT'S WHEN THE PLAYER HATING STARTS.

"

"

I CAN'T EVER SEE ME WASTING MY TIME OR MY TALENT TO DISRESPECT ANOTHER BLACK MAN.

"

On Faith Evans:

"

WHEN I FIRST SAW HER, SHE WAS KILLING ME WITH THOSE EYES. I ROLLED UP TO HER AND SAID 'YOU'RE THE TYPE OF GIRL I WOULD MARRY.' ...

... SHE SAID, 'WHY DON'T YOU?'
SO I WAS LIKE, 'F**K IT, IT'S ON.'
WE HAD ONLY KNOWN EACH
OTHER EIGHT DAYS.

"

"

I HOLD GRUDGES BUT I CAN'T HATE NOBODY, THAT'S NOT MY NATURE.

"

"

I MAY BE A BIG, BLACK, UGLY DUDE; BUT I GOT STYLE. I KINDA UPLIFTED BIG BLACK UGLY DUDES FOR REAL.

"

"

I GOT TO GO WHERE THE DOUGH IS.

"

"

I'M REALLY NO DIFFERENT THAN ANYBODY ELSE, I SAY GROW FROM YOUR MISTAKES AND HOPEFULLY YOU CAN STAND THE REPERCUSSIONS.

"

"

**I'M JUST REALISING
THAT NOTHING PROTECTS
YOU FROM THE INEVITABLE.
IF SOMETHING'S GOING TO
HAPPEN, IT'S GONNA HAPPEN,
NO MATTER WHAT YOU DO …**

... IT'S CRAZY FOR ME TO EVEN THINK THAT A RAPPER CAN'T GET KILLED JUST BECAUSE HE RAPS. THAT S**T CAN HAPPEN.

"

"

WHAT I'M DOING NOW IS RIGHT. I'M TAKING CARE OF MY MOTHER, MY KIDS, AND MY PEERS. IT'S LEGAL, AND I'M USING A TALENT THAT I HAVE TO EXPRESS MYSELF AND GET PAID.

"

"

WHEN I GOT INTO THAT
CAR ACCIDENT, I WAS IN THE
HOSPITAL FOR TWO OR THREE
MONTHS AND IT KIND OF MADE
ME ABLE TO SIT DOWN AND SAY,
'BIG, YOU MOVING TOO FAST.
IT'S TIME FOR S**T TO CHANGE.'

"

"

I'M GONNA DEAL THE CARDS OF MY OWN FATE. I'M GONNA CHEAT. I GOT TO, MAN.

"

"

NEGATIVITY JUST BRINGS FAILURE, YOU KNOW.

"

"

**I COULD NEVER SEE MYSELF
MOVING IN THE SUBURBS.
IT AIN'T GOING TO BE RIGHT,
AND THE LYRICS ARE GOING
TO BE SOUNDIN' NASTY.
I KNOW IT …**

**... THERE WON'T BE NOTHING
TO RAP ABOUT EXCEPT
THE BIRDS.**

"

"

**PEOPLE ARE GONNA
ATTACK ANYONE THAT'S
A LARGE FIGURE; THEY DID
IT TO JORDAN, THEY DID IT
TO TYSON, THEY'RE GONNA
ATTACK YOU IF YOU'RE ON
TOP. IT'S YOUR JOB TO
BOB AND WEAVE.**

"

On Tupac:

"

TUPAC, AT ONE POINT, WAS MY GOD. HE WAS FUNNY AS A MOTHERF*ER TOO. PEOPLE DON'T KNOW THAT.**

"

BIG FACTS

BIGGIE'S TEACHER TOLD HIM THAT HE WAS PROBABLY GOING TO BE A **GARBAGE COLLECTOR** WHEN HE GREW UP.

BIGGIE MARRIED FAITH EVANS

EIGHT DAYS

AFTER THEY HAD MET EACH OTHER.

BIGGIE WAS ARRESTED

SEVEN
TIMES

OVER THE COURSE OF HIS LIFE.

BIG FACTS

BIGGIE HANDED
OUT COPIES OF

READY TO DIE

ON CASSETTE
TO HUNDREDS
OF PEOPLE LINING
UP OUTSIDE HIS
HOUSE.

BIGGIE WENT TO THE GEORGE WESTINGHOUSE INFORMATION TECHNOLOGY SCHOOL...

THE SAME SCHOOL AS
BUSTA RHYMES, DMX AND JAY Z.'

TUPAC REPORTEDLY BOUGHT BIGGIE HIS FIRST ROLEX.

THE NAME
BIGGIE SMALLS
CAME FROM A CHARACTER IN THE 1975 GANGSTER FILM
LET'S DO IT AGAIN.

IN 2015, BILLBOARD NAMED BIGGIE AS **THE GREATEST RAPPER OF ALL TIME.**

BIGGIE'S FIRST STAGE NAME WAS MC QUEST.

BIGGIE SIGNED CAM'RON WHILE BIGGIE WAS IN BED WITH TWO GIRLS AND A BROKEN LEG.

BIGGIE HAS SOLD OVER 17 MILLION ALBUMS IN THE US.

IN THE BIOPIC ABOUT HIS LIFE, **NOTORIOUS,** BIGGIE'S SON, **CHRISTOPHER WALLACE JR.,** PLAYS BIGGIE AS A YOUNG BOY.

BIGGIE STARTED DEALING DRUGS AROUND THE AGE OF 12.

BIGGIE HAD STARTED A PLUS-SIZED CLOTHING LABEL CALLED **BROOKLYN MINT** JUST BEFORE HE DIED.

BIGGIE WAS NOMINATED FOR FOUR GRAMMY AWARDS.

BIGGIE WAS 6 FOOT AND 3 INCHES TALL.

LIFE AFTER DEATH IS CERTIFIED DIAMOND – MEANING IT HAS SOLD OVER **10 MILLION UNITS.**

Sources

'Biggie Smalls on Sway in the morning Last interview he did in L.A', 2016, *BLACK&WHITE*, youtube.com – p. 11

'How Much Did Biggie Smalls Weigh Throughout His Life? And How Tall Was He?', 2018, *Classic Hip Hop Magazine*, classichiphopmagazine.com – p. 92

'Notorious B.I.G Facts: 20 Things You Didn't Know About The Hip-Hop Legend', *Capital Xtra,* capitalxtra.com – p. 76, p. 77, p. 78, pp. 80–81, p. 82, p. 83, p. 85

'Notorious B.I.G Interview Aired March.12.1997', 1997, *Rap City,* youtube.com – p. 24, pp. 26–27, p. 33, pp. 36–37, p. 39, p. 42, pp. 46–47, pp. 50–51, p. 52, p. 62, p. 69, p. 90

'Notorious B.I.G. Speaks on 2Pac Beef in Unreleased 1996 Interview', 2012, *XXL,* xxlmag.com – p. 43, p. 55

'The 10 Best Rappers of All Time', 2015, *Billboard,* billboard.com – p. 84

'The Notorious B.I.G. - Last Interview on KYLD 107.7 FM, San Francisco [March 5, 1997]', 2014, *Felix Montana,* youtube.com – p. 38, p. 54, p. 72

Cepeda, R. 2004, *And It Don't Stop: The Best American Hip-Hop Journalism of the Last 25 Years,* Farra, Straus and Giroux – p. 10, p. 12, p. 13, pp. 14–15, pp. 16–17, pp. 20–21, p. 22, p. 23, p. 25, pp. 30–31, p. 32, p. 34–35, p. 44, p. 45, pp. 48–49, pp. 58–59, p. 60, p. 61, p. 63, pp. 64–65, p. 66, p. 67, p. 68, p. 73

Dandridge-Lemco, B. 2017, 'Puff Daddy, Nas, And More Pay Homage To Notorious B.I.G. On The 20th Anniversary Of His Death', *Fader,* thefader.com – p. 5

Davey, J. 2017, '20 Facts You May Not Know About The Notorious B.I.G', *Highsnobiety,* highsnobiety.com – p. 79, p. 86

Nelson, H. 2016, 'New Again: The Notorious B.I.G.', *Interview magazine,* interviewmagazine.com – p. 53

Notorious (2009), *IMDB,* imdb.com – p. 88

Pocklington, R. 2017, "WE MISS YOU B.I.G." P Diddy remembers The Notorious B.I.G. 20 years after his death', *The Sun,* thesun.co.uk – p. 93

Toure, 1994, 'POP MUSIC; Biggie Smalls, Rap's Man of the Moment', *The New York Times,* nytimes.com – pp. 70–71, p. 89

Pocket Biggie Wisdom

Published in 2019 by Hardie Grant Books,
an imprint of Hardie Grant Publishing

Hardie Grant Books (London)
5th & 6th Floors
52–54 Southwark Street
London SE1 1UN

Hardie Grant Books (Melbourne)
Building 1, 658 Church Street
Richmond, Victoria 3121

hardiegrantbooks.com

British Library Cataloguing-in-Publication Data. A catalogue record for this book is available from the British Library.

ISBN: 978-1-78488-317-1

Publishing Director: Kate Pollard
Junior Editor: Bex Fitzsimons
Design: Jim Green
Cover Illustrator: Michele Rosenthal

Colour Reproduction by p2d
Printed and bound in China by Leo Paper Products Ltd.

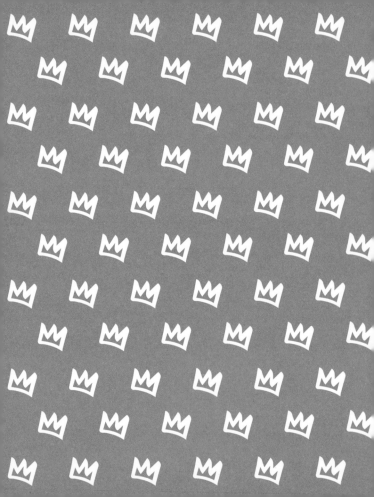